Shadow Warriors: Modern-Day Mercenaries in Action

lf Tucker

Shadow Warriors: Modern-Day Mercenaries in Action

Table Of Contents

Chapter 1: The History of Mercenaries	3
Early Mercenary Armies	3
Renaissance Mercenaries	3
Mercenaries in the Modern Era	4
Chapter 2: Modern-Day Mercenaries	5
The Rise of Private Military Companies	5
The Role of Mercenaries in Modern Conflicts	6
The Ethics of Hiring Mercenaries	7
Chapter 3: Mercenary Training and Tactics	8
Basic Training for Mercenaries	8

Shadow Warriors: Modern-Day Mercenaries in Action

Specialized Training for Mercenaries	9
Mercenary Tactics on the Battlefield	10
Chapter 4: Mercenary Companies and Organizations	**11**
Leading Mercenary Companies	11
The Role of Mercenary Organizations in Conflict Zones	12
The Future of Mercenary Companies	13
Chapter 5: Mercenaries in Action	**14**
Mercenaries in Iraq and Afghanistan	14
Mercenaries in Africa	15
Mercenaries in Latin America	16
Chapter 6: The Life of a Mercenary	**17**

Shadow Warriors: Modern-Day Mercenaries in Action

The Recruitment Process	17
Pay and Benefits for Mercenaries	17
The Challenges and Dangers of Being a Mercenary	18
Chapter 7: The Future of Mercenaries	19
The Impact of Technology on Mercenaries	19
The Role of Mercenaries in Future Conflicts	20
The Pros and Cons of Hiring Mercenaries.	21

Chapter 1: The History of Mercenaries

Early Mercenary Armies

Early Mercenary Armies

Mercenaries have a long and storied history dating back to ancient times. In fact, the first recorded use of mercenary armies can be traced back to the late 8th century BC when Greek mercenaries were hired by the Egyptian pharaohs to fight in their wars.

Throughout history, mercenaries have been used by various nations and kingdoms to supplement their armies. They were often used to fill gaps in military skills and numbers, or to provide specialized services such as siege warfare.

In medieval Europe, knights and soldiers of fortune were hired by lords and kings to fight in their wars. These mercenaries were often paid in gold or land and were known for their prowess in battle.

During the Renaissance, the use of mercenaries became more widespread. The Italian city-states were particularly known for their use of mercenary armies. These armies were composed of soldiers from various European countries and were hired by the city-states to fight in their wars.

Shadow Warriors: Modern-Day Mercenaries in Action

One of the most famous mercenary armies of the Renaissance was the Swiss Guard. This army was hired by the pope to protect the Vatican and was composed of Swiss soldiers known for their discipline and loyalty.

In the 19th and 20th centuries, mercenary armies were used by colonial powers to fight in their colonies. These armies were often composed of soldiers from other colonies or from Europe. They were used to suppress uprisings and rebellions and to protect the interests of the colonial powers.

Today, mercenary armies are still in use around the world. They are often hired by governments or corporations to provide security in conflict zones or to protect valuable assets such as oil fields or mines.

Mercenary armies are often criticized for their lack of loyalty and morality. However, many argue that they provide a necessary service in today's world where traditional armies are often tied up with bureaucracy and politics.

Regardless of one's opinion on mercenary armies, it is clear that they have played an important role in history and continue to play a role in modern-day conflicts.

Renaissance Mercenaries

Shadow Warriors: Modern-Day Mercenaries in Action

The Renaissance period was a time of great change in Europe. It was a time when art, literature, and science flourished, and new ideas and innovations were introduced. The Renaissance also saw the rise of the mercenary soldier, who played a crucial role in the armies of the day.

Renaissance mercenaries were soldiers who were hired by armies or individual rulers to fight in wars. They were often foreigners who had military experience and were willing to fight for pay. Mercenaries were used extensively during the Renaissance period because many rulers did not have standing armies, and those who did could not always rely on them to fight.

One of the most famous Renaissance mercenaries was the German Landsknecht. The Landsknecht were a type of mercenary soldier who were known for their distinctive clothing and their brutal fighting style. They wore brightly colored clothes, often with slashed sleeves and puffed pants, and carried long pikes and swords. The Landsknecht were feared by their enemies for their ferocity in battle.

Another famous Renaissance mercenary was the Swiss mercenary. The Swiss were known for their disciplined fighting style and were considered some of the best soldiers of the time. They were hired by many European rulers, including the French and the English, and played a key role in many battles.

Shadow Warriors: Modern-Day Mercenaries in Action

Mercenaries during the Renaissance were not just hired for their fighting skills. They were also often used for espionage and sabotage. Mercenaries were skilled at infiltrating enemy camps and gathering information, and they were also capable of sabotaging enemy fortifications and supplies.

Despite their importance in Renaissance armies, mercenaries were not always trusted or respected. Many people saw them as unscrupulous and unreliable, and they were often treated poorly by their employers. However, for many mercenaries, the pay and the opportunity to see the world were worth the risks.

Today, the use of mercenaries is still controversial, but they continue to play a role in modern warfare. Mercenary companies and organizations exist all over the world, and many offer specialized training and tactics for those interested in pursuing a career as a modern-day mercenary. Whether or not we agree with their use, mercenaries have been an integral part of warfare for centuries, and their legacy continues to be felt today.

Mercenaries in the Modern Era

Mercenaries in the Modern Era

Shadow Warriors: Modern-Day Mercenaries in Action

The use of mercenaries has a long and storied history that dates back to ancient times. However, the modern era has seen a significant evolution in the role of mercenaries and the tactics they employ. Today, mercenaries are hired by governments, private companies, and even non-governmental organizations to provide security, protection, and military support.

Historical Mercenaries

Historically, mercenaries were often viewed as little more than hired guns. They were hired by monarchs, city-states, and other entities to provide a military force when needed. These mercenaries were often from foreign lands and were motivated primarily by money. They were renowned for their skill and their willingness to fight to the death, but they were also seen as untrustworthy and prone to double-crossing their employers.

Modern-Day Mercenaries

In the modern era, mercenaries have taken on a different role. Today, they are often hired by private companies or NGOs to provide security and protection in volatile regions of the world. These modern-day mercenaries are typically highly trained professionals who are motivated by a sense of duty and a desire to protect others. They often work in dangerous environments and are frequently called upon to provide support to military operations.

Mercenary Training and Tactics

Shadow Warriors: Modern-Day Mercenaries in Action

The training and tactics employed by modern-day mercenaries are highly specialized and often tailored to the specific needs of their clients. They typically undergo extensive physical and mental training to prepare them for the rigors of operating in hostile environments. Their tactics are designed to be highly effective while minimizing the risk of collateral damage.

Mercenary Companies and Organizations

There are numerous companies and organizations that specialize in providing mercenary services. These companies typically employ highly trained professionals who have experience in military and law enforcement operations. They often work closely with their clients to develop customized solutions that meet their specific needs.

Conclusion

The use of mercenaries in the modern era has evolved significantly from its historical roots. Today, mercenaries are highly trained professionals who are motivated by a sense of duty and a desire to protect others. They provide a valuable service to governments, private companies, and NGOs in volatile regions of the world where security and protection are paramount. With their specialized training and tactics, modern-day mercenaries are a vital component of the global security landscape.

Chapter 2: Modern-Day Mercenaries

The Rise of Private Military Companies

The Rise of Private Military Companies

Private military companies, also known as PMCs, have been on the rise in recent years. These companies are made up of hired guns, ex-military personnel, and other highly trained professionals who are paid to provide security and military services to governments, corporations, and other organizations around the world.

The roots of the modern private military industry can be traced back to the early 1990s, when a number of former military personnel began offering security and training services to governments and other clients. These early PMCs were small and often operated in a legal gray area, but they quickly gained a reputation for being highly effective and efficient.

As the demand for private military services grew, more and more companies entered the market. Today, there are dozens of large PMCs operating around the world, with many more smaller firms providing niche services in specific regions or industries.

Shadow Warriors: Modern-Day Mercenaries in Action

The rise of private military companies has been driven by a number of factors. One of the key drivers is the increasing demand for security services in an uncertain and dangerous world. With governments often unable or unwilling to provide the necessary security for their citizens and businesses, private military companies have stepped in to fill the gap.

Another factor is the relative affordability of private military services compared to traditional military forces. Private military companies are often able to provide the same level of security and military capability as a national army or police force, but at a fraction of the cost.

Despite their growing popularity, private military companies are not without controversy. Critics argue that they operate in a legal gray area and are not subject to the same level of oversight and accountability as traditional military forces. There have also been incidents of PMCs engaging in unethical or illegal behavior, such as the infamous Blackwater incident in Iraq.

Despite these concerns, private military companies are likely to continue to play an important role in the world of security and military affairs. As the demand for security services continues to grow, PMCs will likely become an increasingly common sight on the world stage. Whether this is a positive or negative development remains to be seen, but there is no doubt that the rise of private military companies has had a profound impact on the world of mercenaries and military affairs.

The Role of Mercenaries in Modern Conflicts

The Role of Mercenaries in Modern Conflicts

Mercenaries have a storied history, dating back to ancient times when they were hired to fight battles for kings and emperors. Today, mercenaries still play a vital role in modern conflicts around the world. From private military contractors hired by governments to security personnel protecting oil rigs and other critical infrastructure, mercenaries are an important part of the global security landscape.

One of the primary roles of mercenaries in modern conflicts is as trainers and advisors. Many countries lack the military expertise and experience required to effectively fight modern wars. This is where mercenaries come in. They can provide training and advice to local forces, helping them to become more effective in combat and better able to defend their country against external threats.

Another role mercenaries play is as security personnel. In many conflict zones, there are a variety of threats to people and property. Mercenaries can provide security for individuals, organizations, and businesses that are at risk. This can include protecting oil rigs, mines, and other critical infrastructure from attack, as well as providing close protection for VIPs and other high-value targets.

Mercenaries can also play a role in direct combat. In some cases, governments may hire private military contractors to provide additional firepower in a conflict. These mercenaries are trained and equipped to fight in some of the most dangerous environments in the world, and can be an important asset in the fight against terrorism and other threats.

Of course, the use of mercenaries in modern conflicts is not without controversy. Many people view them as mercenaries for hire, motivated solely by money rather than a sense of duty or patriotism. Additionally, there are concerns about the lack of accountability and oversight of mercenaries, who may operate outside the normal rules of engagement and international law.

Despite these concerns, however, mercenaries continue to play a vital role in modern conflicts. Whether as trainers, advisors, or combat troops, they provide a valuable resource for governments and other organizations operating in some of the world's most dangerous regions. As such, it is likely that their role in global security will only continue to grow in the years to come.

The Ethics of Hiring Mercenaries

The Ethics of Hiring Mercenaries

Shadow Warriors: Modern-Day Mercenaries in Action

The use of mercenaries, or hired soldiers, has a long and controversial history dating back to ancient times. From the Greeks and Romans to modern-day private military companies, mercenaries have been utilized for various reasons ranging from supplementing existing military forces to carrying out covert operations.

However, the use of mercenaries raises ethical questions. Is it morally justifiable to hire individuals to fight on behalf of a country or organization for profit? Should the use of mercenaries be regulated or banned altogether?

One argument in favor of hiring mercenaries is that they can be more cost-effective than maintaining a standing army. Governments or organizations may not have the resources to recruit, train, and equip their own soldiers, so hiring mercenaries can be a practical solution. Additionally, mercenaries may have specialized skills and expertise that are not readily available in a regular military force.

However, opponents of hiring mercenaries argue that it is morally wrong to profit from war and that it undermines the principles of duty and patriotism. They also argue that mercenaries may be more likely to engage in human rights abuses or other unethical behavior because they are not bound by the same codes of conduct as regular soldiers.

Furthermore, the use of mercenaries can raise legal and diplomatic concerns. International laws and conventions prohibit the use of mercenaries in armed conflicts, and hiring mercenaries can be seen as a violation of national sovereignty. Additionally, if mercenaries commit atrocities or violate human rights, it can damage diplomatic relations and harm a country's reputation.

Ultimately, the decision to hire mercenaries is a complex one that requires careful consideration of the potential risks and benefits. It is important to weigh the ethical, legal, and diplomatic implications of using mercenaries and to ensure that they are held accountable for any wrongful actions.

In conclusion, the use of mercenaries remains a controversial and divisive issue. While they can offer certain advantages, the ethical concerns must be carefully considered before hiring them. It is important to ensure that any use of mercenaries is conducted within the boundaries of international law and that they are held accountable for their actions.

Chapter 3: Mercenary Training and Tactics

Basic Training for Mercenaries

Basic Training for Mercenaries

Shadow Warriors: Modern-Day Mercenaries in Action

The life of a mercenary can be both exciting and dangerous. That is why it is essential to undergo rigorous training before venturing into the field. Basic training for mercenaries is not only about mastering the art of combat, but it also involves physical and mental preparation.

Physical Training

Physical fitness is the foundation of any successful mercenary. A mercenary must be able to withstand the rigors of the field, which often requires long hours of standing, running, and carrying heavy equipment. Physical training should include cardio exercises, weight training, and endurance training. A mercenary should also be proficient in hand-to-hand combat, martial arts, and weapons handling, to ensure their safety and that of their team.

Mental Training

Mental toughness is equally important for a mercenary. A mercenary must be able to withstand the psychological stress of combat, including the possibility of injury or death. Mental training should include stress management, decision making under pressure, and emotional control. A mercenary must be able to stay focused and composed even in the most challenging situations.

Tactical Training

Tactical training is the backbone of any successful mercenary operation. A mercenary should be able to operate in various environments, including urban, jungle, and desert terrain. Tactical training should include navigation, communication, and teamwork. A mercenary should be able to work with their team to achieve their objectives while minimizing risks.

Conclusion

Basic training for mercenaries is essential for success in the field. Physical, mental, and tactical training are all critical components of a well-rounded mercenary. It is not enough to be physically fit or mentally tough; a mercenary must possess all these qualities to be a successful warrior. A well-trained mercenary is an asset to any organization and can help to achieve the mission objectives while ensuring the safety and security of all involved.

Specialized Training for Mercenaries

Specialized Training for Mercenaries

Mercenaries have been around since ancient times, and their presence has only increased in modern times. These soldiers of fortune are hired by governments, private companies, and individuals to carry out tasks that regular military personnel cannot or will not undertake. As such, they require specialized training to be able to carry out such missions.

Shadow Warriors: Modern-Day Mercenaries in Action

Historically, mercenaries were hired for their combat skills, with little regard to their training. However, as the nature of warfare has changed over the years, so too has the training of mercenaries. Today, specialized training for mercenaries includes a wide range of skills, including combat tactics, specialized weaponry, and survival techniques.

Modern-day mercenaries often undergo training similar to that of regular military personnel, with some key differences. For example, they may receive additional training in specific areas, such as urban warfare, close-quarters combat, and counter-terrorism. They may also receive language training, as many missions require them to operate in foreign countries.

Mercenary training often emphasizes agility and flexibility, as well as adaptability to changing environments. Mercenaries must be able to quickly assess situations and respond accordingly, often with limited resources. They must also be able to work independently, as well as part of a team.

In addition to combat training, mercenaries may also receive specialized training in other areas, such as intelligence gathering and analysis, negotiation, and diplomacy. These skills are essential for carrying out missions that require more than just brute force.

Shadow Warriors: Modern-Day Mercenaries in Action

There are many companies and organizations that specialize in providing training for mercenaries. These companies often employ former military personnel or other experts in the field. They may offer a wide range of training programs, from basic combat training to specialized courses in specific areas.

Overall, specialized training for mercenaries is essential for ensuring that they are able to carry out their missions safely and effectively. As the nature of warfare continues to evolve, so too will the training of mercenaries. However, one thing remains constant: the need for highly skilled and adaptable soldiers of fortune.

Mercenary Tactics on the Battlefield

Mercenary Tactics on the Battlefield

Mercenaries have been around since ancient times. They were once the backbone of many armies and were respected for their fighting skills. Even today, mercenaries are still active on the battlefield, fighting for whoever pays them the most. However, the tactics they use on the battlefield have evolved along with modern warfare.

One of the most important tactics mercenaries use is to blend in with the local population. They often dress like the locals, learn the language, and use their knowledge of the terrain to their advantage. This helps them to move around unnoticed and gather information about the enemy.

Shadow Warriors: Modern-Day Mercenaries in Action

Another important tactic is to use surprise attacks. Mercenaries often use hit-and-run tactics, ambushing their enemies and disappearing before they can be caught. This can be especially effective against a larger, better-equipped force.

Mercenaries also rely heavily on technology. They use advanced weapons, communication devices, and surveillance equipment to gain an edge over their enemies. They also use drones and other unmanned aerial vehicles to gather intelligence and strike targets from a distance.

Training is another important aspect of mercenary tactics. They train rigorously in various forms of combat, including hand-to-hand combat, marksmanship, and explosives. They also learn how to work as a team and adapt to changing situations on the battlefield.

Mercenary companies and organizations also play a crucial role in their success. These companies provide logistical support, intelligence gathering, and other services that allow mercenaries to operate more efficiently. They also provide training and equipment to ensure that their mercenaries are well-prepared for any situation.

Historical mercenaries were often seen as ruthless and unscrupulous, but modern-day mercenaries operate under a strict code of conduct. They adhere to international laws and regulations, and they only engage in combat when they are authorized to do so.

In conclusion, mercenary tactics have evolved along with modern warfare. Today's mercenaries use a combination of traditional and modern tactics, including blending in with the local population, surprise attacks, technology, training, and support from their companies. While they may still be seen as controversial, they play an important role in modern-day conflicts.

Chapter 4: Mercenary Companies and Organizations

Leading Mercenary Companies

Leading Mercenary Companies

Mercenaries have been a part of warfare for centuries, and in today's global landscape, they continue to play a vital role in the security industry. These highly skilled professionals are often employed by governments, corporations, and private individuals to provide security and protection, conduct special operations, and carry out various other tasks.

While there are countless mercenary companies and organizations operating worldwide, some stand out as leaders in the field. These companies have a long history of successful operations, highly trained personnel, and a reputation for professionalism and excellence.

Shadow Warriors: Modern-Day Mercenaries in Action

One such company is Blackwater, which was founded in 1997 by Erik Prince. Blackwater gained widespread notoriety during the Iraq War, where its personnel were involved in several high-profile incidents, including the Nisour Square massacre. Despite this controversy, Blackwater continued to operate and was eventually rebranded as Academi. Today, Academi provides a range of security services to governments, corporations, and individuals around the world.

Another leading mercenary company is Aegis Defence Services, which was founded in 2002 by former British Army officer Tim Spicer. Aegis specializes in providing security and risk management services to governments and corporations in conflict zones. Its personnel are highly trained and experienced in a range of disciplines, including close protection, intelligence gathering, and logistics.

DynCorp International is another major player in the mercenary industry. Founded in 1946, DynCorp has a long history of providing military and security services to governments around the world. Today, the company provides a range of services, including aviation support, logistics, and training.

These are just a few examples of the leading mercenary companies operating today. Each of these companies has a unique history and approach to the work they do, but they all share a commitment to excellence and professionalism.

Shadow Warriors: Modern-Day Mercenaries in Action

For those interested in pursuing a career in the mercenary industry, it's important to research and carefully consider the companies and organizations you may work for. Look for companies with a strong track record of success, experienced leadership, and a commitment to ethical and legal practices.

In addition to working for established companies, some mercenary professionals choose to work as independent contractors or start their own companies. This can be a challenging and rewarding path, but it requires a high level of skill, experience, and business acumen.

Whether you're interested in working for an established mercenary company or striking out on your own, the mercenary industry offers a wealth of opportunities for those with the right skills and mindset. With the right training and experience, you can become a highly sought-after professional in this exciting and dynamic field.

The Role of Mercenary Organizations in Conflict Zones

The Role of Mercenary Organizations in Conflict Zones

Shadow Warriors: Modern-Day Mercenaries in Action

Mercenary organizations have been a part of warfare for centuries. They have been employed by various nations and factions to fight in wars and conflicts that they would otherwise be unable to win. The use of mercenary organizations has been controversial, with many arguing that it is unethical and immoral to hire individuals to fight for money. However, there are also those who argue that mercenary organizations can be a valuable asset in conflict zones.

Historically, mercenary organizations have been used by nations to supplement their own armies. These organizations were often made up of experienced soldiers who were hired to fight for a specific cause. Many of these historical mercenary organizations were famous for their bravery and skill in battle. For example, the Swiss Guards were hired by the French monarchy to protect the king and his family during the French Revolution. They fought bravely but were ultimately defeated, with most of them losing their lives.

In modern times, mercenary organizations have evolved to become more sophisticated and specialized. These organizations are now made up of highly trained individuals who have experience in a variety of fields, including military, law enforcement, and intelligence. They are often hired by governments, corporations, and other organizations to provide security, training, and other services in conflict zones.

Shadow Warriors: Modern-Day Mercenaries in Action

One of the main roles of mercenary organizations in conflict zones is to provide security. This can involve protecting individuals, buildings, and other assets from attack. Mercenary organizations are often hired by corporations operating in conflict zones to provide security for their employees and assets. They are also hired by governments to provide security for foreign dignitaries and embassy personnel.

Another important role of mercenary organizations in conflict zones is to provide training and support for local forces. Many conflict zones are characterized by weak or non-existent local security forces. Mercenary organizations can provide training and support to these forces, helping them to become more effective in their efforts to maintain peace and security.

Mercenary organizations also play a role in providing intelligence and other information to their clients. This can include information on the location and activities of enemy forces, as well as information on local political and social dynamics.

In conclusion, while the use of mercenary organizations in conflict zones is controversial, there are many arguments that suggest they can be a valuable asset. Historical mercenary organizations have been famous for their bravery and skill in battle, while modern-day mercenary organizations provide valuable services such as security, training, and intelligence gathering. As such, mercenary organizations will likely continue to play a role in conflict zones for the foreseeable future.

The Future of Mercenary Companies

The Future of Mercenary Companies

The concept of mercenary companies has been around for centuries, and they have been used for a variety of purposes, from supplementing armies to providing security for corporations and individuals. However, the future of mercenary companies is uncertain, as the world becomes increasingly complex and the demands placed on them change.

Historically, mercenary companies were often used by countries that lacked the resources to maintain a standing army. These companies were made up of soldiers who were hired to fight for the highest bidder, and they were often seen as a necessary evil. However, in recent years, the use of mercenaries has become more controversial, as they are seen as a potential threat to national security and as a cause for political instability.

Modern-day mercenary companies have evolved to meet the changing demands of the world. While some companies still provide traditional military services, others have branched out into providing security services for corporations and individuals. These companies may provide security for high-profile events, protect critical infrastructure, or provide personal protection services for individuals.

Shadow Warriors: Modern-Day Mercenaries in Action

The future of mercenary companies is likely to be shaped by a number of factors. One of the biggest factors will be the changing nature of warfare. As technology advances, the way wars are fought is changing, and mercenary companies will need to adapt to these changes if they are to remain relevant.

Another factor that will shape the future of mercenary companies is the increasing demand for security services. As the world becomes more dangerous, corporations and individuals will need to hire security professionals to protect themselves and their assets. This demand for security services is likely to grow in the coming years, and mercenary companies are well-positioned to meet this demand.

Finally, the future of mercenary companies will be shaped by the changing political landscape. As countries become more inward-looking and nationalist, the demand for foreign mercenaries may decrease. However, as the threat of terrorism and other non-state actors continues to grow, the demand for mercenary companies that can provide security services may increase.

In conclusion, the future of mercenary companies is uncertain, but they are likely to continue to play an important role in the world. As the demands placed on them change, they will need to adapt and evolve to remain relevant. Whether they are providing traditional military services or security services for corporations and individuals, mercenary companies are likely to be a key player in the security landscape for years to come.

Chapter 5: Mercenaries in Action

Mercenaries in Iraq and Afghanistan

The use of mercenaries in Iraq and Afghanistan has been a controversial topic since the beginning of the wars. Private military companies (PMCs) were brought in to fill a void left by the military, but their actions have been scrutinized by the media and politicians alike.

One of the most well-known PMCs in Iraq was Blackwater, which was founded by Erik Prince in 1997. Blackwater provided security services for the US State Department and other government agencies, but their actions came under fire after the Nisour Square massacre in 2007. Blackwater employees opened fire on civilians, killing 17 people and injuring 20 others. Four of the employees were later convicted of manslaughter charges.

In Afghanistan, PMCs were used for a variety of tasks, including providing security for convoys and military installations. One of the largest PMCs in Afghanistan was DynCorp, which provided training for Afghan security forces and performed maintenance on military equipment. However, DynCorp also faced controversy when one of its employees was accused of raping an Afghan boy in 2009.

Shadow Warriors: Modern-Day Mercenaries in Action

The use of mercenaries in Iraq and Afghanistan has raised questions about their effectiveness and accountability. While PMCs were able to fill a void left by the military, their actions were not always in line with the rules of engagement or international law. Additionally, the lack of oversight and accountability for PMCs has led to concerns about human rights violations and war crimes.

Despite the controversies surrounding the use of PMCs in Iraq and Afghanistan, the industry continues to thrive. Many former military personnel are drawn to the high-paying jobs and opportunities for adventure and excitement. However, those considering a career as a mercenary should be aware of the risks and potential consequences of their actions.

In order to be successful as a mercenary, individuals must have a strong understanding of military tactics and strategy. They must also be able to adapt to changing situations and work well under pressure. While many PMCs offer training programs, individuals should also seek out additional training and education to expand their skillset.

Overall, the use of mercenaries in Iraq and Afghanistan has had a significant impact on the wars and the military-industrial complex. While there are certainly concerns about their accountability and effectiveness, the industry looks set to continue to play a role in modern warfare.

Mercenaries in Africa

Shadow Warriors: Modern-Day Mercenaries in Action

Africa has been a hotbed for conflict and war for decades, and mercenaries have played a significant role in the region's history. From colonial times to modern-day conflicts, mercenaries have been hired to fight in various African countries, often with devastating consequences.

Historically, mercenaries were used by European powers to colonize Africa and exploit its resources. European powers hired mercenaries to fight against indigenous communities, leading to the loss of countless lives and the displacement of millions of people. In the 20th century, mercenaries were hired by African leaders to fight against other African countries, leading to some of the deadliest conflicts in history.

Today, the use of mercenaries in Africa is still prevalent, with private military companies (PMCs) offering their services to governments and rebel groups alike. These PMCs are often hired to provide security for oil companies, mining operations, and other industries that operate in high-risk areas.

The training and tactics used by modern-day mercenaries are highly specialized and designed to operate in environments where conventional military forces cannot. These tactics include close-quarter combat training, intelligence gathering, and counter-insurgency operations. Mercenaries are also trained in the use of advanced weapons and technologies, including drones and surveillance equipment.

Shadow Warriors: Modern-Day Mercenaries in Action

Mercenary companies and organizations operating in Africa are often controversial, with accusations of human rights abuses and war crimes. The lack of accountability and oversight of these companies has led to concerns about their impact on local communities and the region's stability.

In conclusion, the use of mercenaries in Africa has a long and complicated history, with both positive and negative outcomes. While some argue that mercenaries provide a valuable service in protecting commercial interests and supporting local governments, others believe that they exacerbate conflicts and contribute to instability in the region. It is up to policymakers and the international community to regulate the use of mercenaries and ensure that their actions do not violate human rights or international law.

Mercenaries in Latin America

The use of mercenaries in Latin America has a long and complex history. From the days of the conquistadors to the modern era of drug cartels and political instability, mercenaries have played a pivotal role in the region's conflicts and power struggles.

One of the earliest examples of mercenaries in Latin America can be found in the Spanish conquest of the Aztec and Inca empires. Spanish conquistadors relied heavily on mercenaries from Italy and Germany to bolster their forces and provide specialized skills such as artillery and engineering.

Shadow Warriors: Modern-Day Mercenaries in Action

In the 20th century, mercenaries became more prominent in Latin America as a result of the Cold War. The United States and Soviet Union both sought to influence the region's politics and often used mercenaries as a proxy force. The Bay of Pigs invasion in Cuba and the Contra War in Nicaragua are two prominent examples of this.

Today, mercenaries continue to be a factor in Latin America's conflicts and power struggles. Drug cartels in Mexico and Colombia have been known to hire mercenaries for protection and enforcement. Additionally, political factions in countries such as Venezuela and Nicaragua are suspected of using mercenaries to suppress opposition and maintain power.

Mercenaries in Latin America often come from a variety of backgrounds, including former military personnel, private security contractors, and even criminal organizations. Their training and tactics can vary widely depending on the situation and employer.

Mercenary companies and organizations also play a role in the region. Blackwater (now known as Academi) famously provided security for U.S. officials in Iraq, but also had contracts with the Colombian government to provide training and support for their military and police forces.

The use of mercenaries in Latin America raises ethical questions about accountability and transparency. Unlike regular military forces, mercenaries are not subject to the same rules and regulations and often operate in a legal gray area.

Overall, the role of mercenaries in Latin America is a complex and controversial issue. While they can provide valuable skills and support in certain situations, their use also raises concerns about accountability and human rights.

Chapter 6: The Life of a Mercenary

The Recruitment Process

The recruitment process is a crucial step in building a successful team of mercenaries. It is the first step towards creating a group of skilled and experienced individuals who can work together to accomplish a mission.

The recruitment process for mercenaries is different from that of regular military personnel. Mercenaries come from all walks of life and have varying levels of experience and skills. Therefore, the recruitment process needs to be tailored to the individual needs of each potential recruit.

The first step in the recruitment process is identifying potential recruits. This can be done through advertising, networking, or word-of-mouth referrals. Once potential recruits are identified, they are screened to determine their level of experience, skills, and suitability for the mission.

Shadow Warriors: Modern-Day Mercenaries in Action

The screening process involves a thorough evaluation of the candidate's training, experience, and background. This includes a review of their military or law enforcement records, as well as a background check. The screening process also includes interviews with the candidate to determine their motivation, commitment, and ability to work in a team environment.

Once a candidate has passed the screening process, they are invited to join the team. This is typically done through a formal contract that outlines the terms of their employment, including their compensation, benefits, and responsibilities.

The training process for mercenaries is typically intensive and focused on preparing them for the specific mission they will be assigned to. This may include language training, weapons training, and survival training. Mercenaries are also trained in tactics and strategy, as well as how to work effectively in a team environment.

Overall, the recruitment process for mercenaries is a complex and challenging process. It requires a significant investment of time and resources to identify, screen, and train the right individuals for the job. However, with the right team in place, mercenaries can be highly effective in achieving their mission objectives and ensuring the safety and security of their clients.

Pay and Benefits for Mercenaries

Pay and Benefits for Mercenaries

Shadow Warriors: Modern-Day Mercenaries in Action

One of the most significant factors that drive people to become mercenaries is the financial reward. Unlike regular soldiers, mercenaries are hired on a contractual basis, and their pay is determined by the length of their contract, the nature of their assignment, and their skills and experience. The amount that mercenaries can earn varies depending on the type of work they are hired for, the location of their assignment, and the level of risk involved. In this subchapter, we will explore the pay and benefits that mercenaries can expect to receive.

Historically, mercenaries were paid a fixed amount of money, known as the "soldier's wage," which was often meager compared to what regular soldiers received. However, in modern times, the pay and benefits for mercenaries have significantly improved, making it a more attractive career option for people with specialized skills and experience. Typically, mercenaries are paid a daily rate, which can range from a few hundred dollars to thousands of dollars, depending on the assignment.

In addition to their daily rate, mercenaries may receive other benefits such as health insurance, life insurance, and retirement benefits. Some mercenary companies also offer their employees bonuses for completing successful missions or for recruiting new members. These bonuses can be substantial and can significantly increase a mercenary's earnings.

The pay and benefits for mercenaries may also be influenced by the level of risk involved in their assignments. For example, a mercenary hired to provide security for a VIP may receive a higher daily rate than one hired to provide security for a construction site. Similarly, a mercenary hired to work in a war zone may receive a higher daily rate than one hired to provide security in a relatively safe area.

In conclusion, the pay and benefits for mercenaries have significantly improved in modern times, making it a viable career option for people with specialized skills and experience. The amount that mercenaries can earn varies depending on the type of work they are hired for, the location of their assignment, and the level of risk involved. While the financial rewards may be attractive, becoming a mercenary requires a unique set of skills and a willingness to work in dangerous and challenging environments.

The Challenges and Dangers of Being a Mercenary

Being a mercenary is a job that comes with a lot of risks and challenges. While it may seem like an exciting and adventurous career, it is important to understand the potential dangers that come with it.

Shadow Warriors: Modern-Day Mercenaries in Action

One of the biggest challenges of being a mercenary is the lack of legal protection. Mercenaries are not recognized as soldiers under international law, which means that they do not enjoy the same protections as regular soldiers. This can make them vulnerable to prosecution and persecution if they are captured or detained by enemy forces.

Another challenge is the high level of physical and mental stress that comes with the job. Mercenaries are often deployed in dangerous and hostile environments, where they must be constantly vigilant and ready to respond to threats. This can take a toll on their physical and mental health, leading to issues such as post-traumatic stress disorder (PTSD) and other mental health problems.

There is also the danger of being caught in the crossfire of conflicts that are not their own. Mercenaries are often hired by governments or private companies to provide security or combat support in areas of conflict. However, they may find themselves caught in the middle of a larger conflict that they have no stake in, which can put them in grave danger.

Finally, there is the danger of being targeted by terrorist groups or other hostile actors. Mercenaries are often seen as symbols of foreign intervention and may be targeted by groups that oppose their presence in a particular region.

In conclusion, being a mercenary is not a job for the faint of heart. It requires a high level of skill, physical and mental toughness, and a willingness to put oneself in harm's way. However, for those who are up to the challenge, it can be a rewarding and exciting career.

Chapter 7: The Future of Mercenaries

The Impact of Technology on Mercenaries

The impact of technology on mercenaries has been profound and has significantly changed the nature of modern-day warfare. The use of advanced technology has made it easier for mercenaries to operate in hostile environments, gather intelligence, and carry out their missions more efficiently.

One of the most significant impacts of technology on modern-day mercenaries is the use of drones. Drones have become an essential tool for modern-day warfare, and mercenaries have been quick to adopt this technology. Drones enable mercenaries to gather intelligence, monitor enemy movements, and carry out targeted strikes without putting their lives at risk.

Shadow Warriors: Modern-Day Mercenaries in Action

Another significant impact of technology on mercenaries is the use of advanced weapons systems. Mercenaries are now able to access state-of-the-art weapons and equipment that were previously only available to national armies. This has made it easier for mercenaries to carry out their missions and has made them more effective on the battlefield.

The use of satellite technology has also had a significant impact on mercenaries. Satellite imagery and communications technology have made it easier for mercenaries to communicate with each other and with their clients. This has enabled them to carry out their missions more efficiently and has made them more effective overall.

The impact of technology on modern-day mercenaries has not been entirely positive, however. The use of advanced technology has also made it easier for governments and other organizations to track and monitor the activities of mercenaries. This has led to increased scrutiny of the industry and has made it harder for mercenaries to operate in certain areas.

Despite these challenges, the impact of technology on modern-day mercenaries has been overwhelmingly positive. The use of advanced technology has made it easier for mercenaries to carry out their missions and has made them more effective on the battlefield. As technology continues to advance, it is likely that the role of mercenaries in modern-day warfare will continue to evolve and adapt to these changes.

The Role of Mercenaries in Future Conflicts

The Role of Mercenaries in Future Conflicts

The use of mercenaries in conflicts is not a new phenomenon. However, their role in future conflicts is likely to change in many ways due to technological advancements, evolving warfare strategies, and shifting political landscapes. In this chapter, we will explore the potential role of mercenaries in future conflicts, and the implications of their involvement.

Historical Mercenaries

Historically, mercenaries were hired by states or individuals to fight wars on their behalf. They were often motivated by financial gain, and were known for their ruthlessness and lack of loyalty. However, the use of mercenaries declined as states developed their own professional armies. Today, the use of mercenaries is largely confined to private military companies (PMCs) and security firms.

Modern-Day Mercenaries

Shadow Warriors: Modern-Day Mercenaries in Action

Modern-day mercenaries are often recruited from military veterans, and are trained to provide a range of services, including security, intelligence gathering, and training. They are often employed by governments, corporations, and individuals who require specialist skills and expertise.

Mercenary Training and Tactics

Mercenaries receive specialized training that prepares them for a range of scenarios, including urban warfare, counter-terrorism, and hostage rescue. They are often equipped with state-of-the-art weapons and technology, and are trained to operate in high-risk environments. Mercenaries also use a range of tactics, including guerrilla warfare, sabotage, and assassination.

Mercenary Companies and Organizations

The use of mercenaries is highly controversial, and there are many organizations that campaign against their use. However, there are also many companies and organizations that provide mercenary services. These include well-known PMCs such as Blackwater and Aegis, as well as smaller, more specialized firms.

The Role of Mercenaries in Future Conflicts

The role of mercenaries in future conflicts is likely to be shaped by a number of factors. Firstly, technological advancements will enable mercenaries to operate more efficiently and effectively in a range of environments. This will include the use of drones, robotics, and cyber warfare.

Secondly, the changing nature of warfare will require mercenaries to adapt to new threats and challenges. This will include the need to operate in urban environments, where conventional military tactics are often not effective.

Finally, the shifting political landscape will also impact the role of mercenaries. As states become more reluctant to engage in direct military action, the use of mercenaries may become more widespread. This will be particularly true in conflicts where there is no clear legal framework or international consensus.

In conclusion, the role of mercenaries in future conflicts is likely to be shaped by a range of factors, including technological advancements, evolving warfare strategies, and shifting political landscapes. While the use of mercenaries is highly controversial, they are likely to continue to play a significant role in conflicts around the world.

The Pros and Cons of Hiring Mercenaries.

Shadow Warriors: Modern-Day Mercenaries in Action

The use of mercenaries, or hired soldiers, has been a topic of debate for centuries. While there are certainly pros and cons to hiring mercenaries, it is important to understand the potential risks and benefits before making a decision to employ them.

Pros:

1. Flexibility: Mercenaries are often more flexible than regular military forces because they can be hired on an as-needed basis. This can be especially useful in situations where the conflict is fluid and rapidly changing.

2. Specialized Skills: Mercenaries often have specialized skills that are not available in regular military forces. For example, they may be experts in a particular type of warfare, such as guerrilla tactics or urban combat.

3. Cost-Effective: In some cases, hiring mercenaries can be more cost-effective than maintaining a permanent military force. This is especially true if the conflict is short-term or if the military force is only needed for a specific operation.

4. Political Plausibility: In some cases, using mercenaries can be more politically plausible than deploying regular military forces. This is because of the perception that mercenaries are less likely to be seen as an occupying force.

Cons:

Shadow Warriors: Modern-Day Mercenaries in Action

1. Unpredictability: Mercenaries are not bound by the same rules and regulations as regular military forces, which can make them unpredictable. This can lead to issues such as rogue behavior or a lack of discipline.

2. Lack of Loyalty: Mercenaries are not necessarily loyal to the country or organization that hires them. This can create issues if the mercenaries become disillusioned or if they are offered a better deal by a different employer.

3. Legal Issues: The use of mercenaries can raise legal issues, particularly if they are hired to operate in a country where they are not welcome. This can lead to accusations of war crimes or other violations of international law.

4. Public Perception: Using mercenaries can be controversial, particularly if the public perceives them as "guns for hire" rather than legitimate soldiers fighting for a cause.

Overall, the decision to hire mercenaries is a complex one that requires careful consideration of the potential risks and benefits. While there are certainly advantages to using hired soldiers, there are also significant downsides that must be taken into account. Ultimately, the decision to use mercenaries should be based on a thorough analysis of the situation, the available resources, and the potential consequences.

www.ingramcontent.com/pod-product-compliance
Lightning Source LLC
Chambersburg PA
CBHW070442010526
44118CB00014B/2154